Take Back Dominion Using the Kingdom Keys Jesus Gave Us

Bridget A. Desiderio

Published by Bdesiderio
Copyright © Bridget A. Desiderio, 2022

All rights reserved. No portion of this book may be reproduced in any form without written permission from the publisher, except as permitted by the United States copyright law.
For permissions contact Bridget A. Desiderio:

Tamaradesi360@gmail.com
Cover by: Crownwriter29@gmail.com

Bible Hub, Expositor's Bible Commentary, 2004-2022
Dr. Kevin Zadai: KevnZadai.com
Warriornotes.netviewshop.com,
2019-2022
Prophet and Revelator Kat Kerr: RevealingHeaven.com, 2022

ISBN 979-8-9867420-1-4

*Take Back Dominion
Using the
Kingdom Keys Jesus
Gave Us*

Bridget A. Desiderio

FOREWORD

Jesus said in Luke 19:13(KJV) 'Occupy until I come.' I believe that it means we are empowered as followers of Jesus, to TAKE BACK DOMINION from any evil around us. This includes our homes, neighborhoods, towns and cities, states, countries, etc. As He said:

> *"Behold, I give you the authority to trample on serpents and scorpions, and over all the power of the enemy, and nothing shall by any means hurt you."* Luke 10:19 (NKJV)

And since we are children, then we are heirs: heirs of God and co-heirs with Christ - Romans 8:17 (BSB)

> *"Be strong and of good courage, do not fear nor be afraid of them; for the LORD your God, He is the One who goes with you. He will not leave you nor forsake you."* Duet 31:6 (NKJV)

This authority gives us the ability to OCCUPY as co-heirs and joint rulers with JESUS in our homes, by using our voices as guided by God's Holy Spirit.

God is calling us to STAND WITH HIM in our areas of influence and for our families! We CAN overcome! That is what this book is intended to help you do!

I pray for all of Heaven to help each of us overcome and take back dominion in our lives! I pray for an open heavenly portal over us and our homes in Jesus' name! All glory be to the Most High God! Amen and amen!

Blessings in Jesus' name!

TABLE OF CONTENTS

FOREWORD 4
TABLE OF CONTENTS 6
CHAPTER ONE 7
   OUR COVENANT WITH GOD 7
CHAPTER TWO 10
   COMMUNION WITH GOD 10
CHAPTER THREE 14
   THE BLOOD OF JESUS 14
CHAPTER FOUR 18
   THE NAME OF JESUS 18
CHAPTER FIVE 20
   THE ANOINTING 20
CHAPTER SIX 23
   THE WORD OF GOD SPOKEN IN FAITH . 23
CHAPTER SEVEN 28
   THE FIRE OF GOD 28
CHAPTER EIGHT 30
   THE LIVING WATER 30
CHAPTER NINE 33
   SPEAKING IN TONGUES 33
CHAPTER TEN 38
   ADDITIONAL KEYS 38

CHAPTER ONE

OUR COVENANT WITH GOD

Our covenant with God started the moment we believed what God said in His word about Jesus! The moment we were saved and born again!

> John 3:16 (ESV) For God so loved the world, that he gave His only Son, that whoever believes in Him should not perish but have eternal life.
>
> 1 Corinthians 11:25 (NIV) In the same way, after supper, He (Jesus) took the cup, saying, 'This cup is the new covenant in My blood.'
>
> Matt 26:28 (NASB) ...for this is My blood of the covenant, which is being poured out for many for the forgiveness of sins.

This Covenant sealed us as Children of God! We are now God's children!

> Galatians 3:26 (ESV) For in Christ Jesus you are all sons of God, through faith.
>
> 1 John 3:1 (ESV) See what kind of love the Father has given to us, that we should be called children of God; and so, we are.
>
> Romans 8:16 (ESV) The Spirit Himself bears witness with our spirit that we are children of God.

So, you know the Covenant with God makes you His child and that means you stand empowered with Jesus! And God honor's His Covenant forever!

> Psalm 89:34 (NASB) I will not violate My covenant, Nor will I alter the utterance of My lips.

Now, say aloud:

> I AM a son (or daughter) of the Most High God and I believe it in Jesus' name!

Say it as many times as you need to until you get it into your mind, soul, and spirit that this IS TRUE!

You ARE a walking son (or daughter) of God Almighty!

You ARE a KING, a co-heir with King Jesus!

You ARE a King of THE KING!

Jesus IS THE KING OF KINGS...and we, the new creatures in Jesus Christ, are the Kings Jesus is KING over! Hallelujah!

Say it often and say it aloud in your house!

Change the atmosphere around you and put the spirit realm on alert that you KNOW you ARE a Child of God by constantly proclaiming it verbally every time you think about it!

Once you have planted this truth in your being and in your home, all will change from 'fear mode' into 'faith mode'! Why? Because Romans 8:31 (AMP) says: What then shall we say to all these things? If God is for us, who can be [successful] against us?

So, start to stand on your Covenant with God by proclaiming you ARE A CHILD OF GOD! Always remember, when you got saved and became a "New Creature in Christ" (2 Corinthians 5:17) your name was written in the Lamb's Book of Life, and all evil MUST obey you!

> Luke 10:20 (KJV) Nevertheless, do not rejoice in this, that the spirits ARE subject to you, but rejoice that your names are written in heaven.

So, here is an example of what I say:

> Father, I am your child and I take full authority over any evil in my home. I command all evil to LEAVE MY HOUSE NOW IN JESUS' NAME! Then I open a door and swing my foot out the door as though I am kicking something outside and then close the door... all as a prophetic act!*[1]

---

[1] *I confess and know that this is my reality.*

CHAPTER TWO

COMMUNION WITH GOD

The next step I take is having Holy Communion with God in my home.

> 1 Corinthians 1:9 (KJV) God is faithful, by whom ye were called unto the fellowship of his Son Jesus Christ our Lord.
>
> John 15:13 (AMP) No one has greater love [nor stronger commitment] than to lay down his own life for his friends.
>
> Romans 6:13 (KJV) ... yield yourselves unto God, as those that are alive from the dead, and your members as instruments of righteousness unto God.

I commune with God daily in my home! I get the pre-filled communion cups and have them ready for my communion time with God!

> John 6:53 (NKJV) Then Jesus said to them, 'Most assuredly, I say to you, unless you eat the flesh of the Son of Man and drink His blood, you have no life in you...

So, I start by taking the communion elements, the bread, and the juice, and say: "Father, I thank you for the communion bread and juice, and I ask you to bless them in Jesus' name. Amen."

Then I break my wafer in half, read 1 Corinthians 11:24, and I say:

'I take and eat; this is your body, Jesus, which was broken for me: I this do in remembrance of you, Jesus, in your name!'

And then I add:

'Because you were wounded for my transgressions, you were bruised for my iniquities; the chastisement for my peace was upon you, and by your stripes, Jesus, I am healed, in your mighty name! Amen!' (Which is Isaiah 53:5 personalized to me).

Then I eat the broken wafer.

Next, I hold up the cup and say:

"This cup is the new covenant in your blood, Jesus. I do this, as often as I drink it, in remembrance of you, Jesus. Amen!" (Which is 1 Corinthians 11:25.)

Then I add:

"Thank you, Jesus, for your blood and by your stripes, I am healed and I accept your healing in your name!"

Amen and amen!

Then I drink from the cup, and I am done.

As an additional tool of taking dominion back, I also do Holy Communion with the land each time I move, or when I buy a property!

How?

First, I thank God for the new place He has given me, then I repent for any and all sins that have been committed on the property, and I ask God to forgive the sins and the sinners.

Then I say:

"I now dedicate this property to you Abba Father, in Jesus' mighty name!" Then I dig a hole in the ground.

Next, I bite a piece of the wafer off, and then I put the other leftover half, in the hole in the ground, as I say this communion prayer:

> "I take and eat; this is your body, Jesus, which was broken for me: I this do in remembrance of you, Jesus, in your name! Because you were wounded for my transgressions, you were bruised for my iniquities; the chastisement for my peace was upon you, and by your stripes, Jesus, I am healed, and this land is healed in your mighty name! Amen!"

Next, I drink half of the cup of juice and pour the remaining juice into the hole in the ground, as I say this communion prayer,

> "This cup is the new covenant in your blood, with me, and with this land, Jesus. I do this in remembrance of you, Jesus. Amen and amen!"

Finally, I verbally bless the land out loud and I cover up the hole.

CHAPTER THREE

THE BLOOD OF JESUS

The next key I use is the most powerful substance to ever exist on our planet, the blood of Jesus!

His blood is so powerful, that when it touched the ground underneath the cross on which Jesus was nailed, it started an earthquake!

The ground literally shook and graves opened and many dead people rose from the dead and came out of their graves!

How do I know this?

> Matthew 27:51-52: (NKJV) Then, behold, the veil of the temple was torn in two from top to bottom; and the earth quaked, and the rocks were split, and the graves were opened; and many bodies of the saints who had fallen asleep were raised;

The blood of Jesus is also so pure, that it was the only element to satisfy the Law! It cleanses us from all sin! It washes away our sins completely!

> Hebrews 9:12-14 (NIV) He did not enter by means of the blood of goats and calves; but He entered the Most Holy Place once for all by His own blood, thus obtaining eternal redemption.

> The blood of goats and bulls and the ashes of a heifer sprinkled on those who are ceremonially unclean sanctify them so that they are outwardly clean.
>
> How much more, then, will the blood of Christ, who through the eternal Spirit offered Himself unblemished to God, cleanse our consciences from acts that lead to death, so that we may serve the living God!

Now think about it, if Jesus' blood is so pure and holy that it satisfies God's law requirement, it must be enormously powerful! And it is!

There is no other matter that is more powerful than the blood of Jesus! Now and forever.

> Hebrews 2:14 (ESV) Since therefore the children share in flesh and blood, He himself likewise partook of the same things, that through death He might destroy the one who has the power of death, that is, the devil.
>
> Hebrews 10:19 (NIV) Therefore, brothers, since we have confidence to enter the holy places by the blood of Jesus.
>
> Revelation 12:11 (ESV) And they have conquered him (satan) by the blood of the Lamb and by the word of their testimony, for they loved not their lives even unto death.

So, we too can apply the blood of Jesus, our Lord, and Savior, to anything we choose to cover from the enemy!

Here is one example; I say:

"Father, I apply the blood of Jesus over my home in Jesus' name! Amen!"

And I say:

"Father, I apply the blood of Jesus over my children, from the tops of their heads to the bottom of their feet in Jesus' name! Amen!"

I apply the blood to everything the Holy Spirit encourages me to cover! It is the same prophetic act that was done by the Jews before Moses led them out of Egypt in Exodus 12:7 (KJV): 'And they shall take of the blood and strike it on the two side posts and on the upper door post of the houses, wherein they shall eat it.'

This was a prophetic act of the Jewish people applying the blood (of Jesus) to protect them! And it worked!

So, I believe that everything done in the bible can be done by us today! That includes spiritually applying the blood of Jesus to everything we want to be protected.

When I bring anything into my home, I cover it in the blood of Jesus to make sure nothing gets into my home undercover.

I say:

"Father, I cover all these items in the blood of Jesus, amen!"

I have also heard people say:

"I cleanse these items for the Kingdom of God in Jesus' name! Amen!"

CHAPTER FOUR

THE NAME OF JESUS

One reason the name of Jesus is powerful is that His name came directly from God in Luke 1:31, 'You will conceive and give birth to a son, and you are to call Him Jesus.'

Another reason is that Jesus was the ONLY person to fight the devil and win!

> Colossians 2:15 (NLT) And having disarmed the powers and authorities, He made a public spectacle of them, triumphing over them (all of hell, satan and the unclean spirits) by the cross.

The name of Jesus is enormously powerful for us today!

I have been told that satan and his demons fear Jesus so much, that they run when they hear the name, Jesus!

Why?

Because they KNOW that Jesus already conquered them!

And when they see and hear us use the name of Jesus,

> Philippians 2:9 (NLT) Therefore God exalted Him to the highest place and gave Him the name above all names,

They run screaming with fear!

So, when I use the name of Jesus, I say:

"Father, I cast out the spirit of fear IN JESUS' NAME! Amen!"

"Father, I take dominion over my home IN JESUS' NAME! Amen!"

Or, if I need Him quickly, I just say:

"Jesus, I need you!"

Or I cry out to him by saying:

"Jesus!"

However, there is one thing we must all remember: Do not misuse the name of Jesus!

> Exodus 20:7 (NIV) You shall not misuse the name of the LORD your God, for the LORD will not hold anyone guiltless who misuses his name.

CHAPTER FIVE

THE ANOINTING

Sometimes we hear about 'The Anointing" but we are not sure exactly what it is.

Well, in scripture it is a few things:

It is His people:

> Psalm 20:6 (NKJV) Now I know that the LORD saves His anointed.

It is boldness and power:

> Luke 4:18 (NIV) The Spirit of the Lord is on me, because he has anointed me to proclaim good news to the poor. He has sent me to proclaim freedom for the prisoners and recovery of sight for the blind, to set the oppressed free,

It is a portion of Him:

> 1 John 2:27 (NASB 1995) As for you, the anointing which you received from Him abides in you, and you have no need for anyone to teach you; but as His anointing teaches you about all things, and is true and is not a lie, and just as it has taught you, you abide in Him.

The Anointing I am referring to as a Kingdom Key and a tool for us to use is the last description -a portion of Him in us!

Since we all know that God IS Love, I like to think of 'the anointing' as liquid love! And I am the vessel that holds His liquid love here on Earth!

And I can release this liquid love-the anointing, any time I choose to, as an act of my will!

I have heard and I believe that each time we release our anointing, we get more!

I equate the anointing inside each of us to this scripture:

> 1 Thessalonians 3:12 (NIV) May the Lord make your love increase and overflow for each other and for everyone else, just as ours does for you.

The more we release God's anointing, the more we get refilled by Him!

And the best part about God's anointing inside of us is that it is a powerful substance to stop the devil's hold on anything, per Isaiah 10:27 which says:

> It shall come to pass in that day That his burden will be taken away from your shoulder, and his yoke from your neck, And the yoke will be destroyed because of the anointing oil.

And as described in MurrayLedger.com:

> Isaiah 10:27 defines anointing as the burden-removing, yoke-destroying power of God. The anointing is what delivers God's people and sets the

captives free. The anointing is literally God on flesh doing what flesh cannot do. It is God's super, added to our 'natural'

So, when I drive by a liquor store, bar, strip club, or the like

I always say:

> "Father, as an act of my will, I release my anointing to break the devil's yoke and to spread your love to all people who go here in Jesus' name! Amen!"

Or I use it this way:

> "Father, as an act of my will, I release your anointing here on this road, so that all who drive on it will feel your love in their lives in Jesus' name! Amen!"

Or I use it as follows:

> "Father, as an act of my will, I release your anointing on my property to soak into the ground and touch every home in my neighborhood; for every house to be flooded by your love and bring forth your peace and harmony here in Jesus' name! Amen!"

CHAPTER SIX

THE WORD OF GOD SPOKEN IN FAITH

As we all know, the most powerful words ever spoken or inspired are literally in the Holy Bible! There are no other words I can think of that are more powerful than the words that came directly from God's heart and mouth!

God's words are so powerful, that I believe Jesus knew it and that's one reason why He only said or did what His Father said or did. He too, knew that nothing was more powerful than God's own words!

> John 14:24 (NASB) The one who does not love Me does not follow My words; and the word which you hear is not Mine, but the Father's who sent Me.
>
> Isaiah 55:11 (KJV) So shall My word be that goes forth from My mouth; It shall not return to Me void, But it shall accomplish what I please, And it shall prosper in the thing for which I sent it.
>
> Ephesians 5:1 (NJKV) Therefore be imitators of God as dear children.

Do you realize that Jesus also only used the written word to defeat satan?

> Mark 4:4 (NKJV) But He answered and said, "**It is written,** 'Man shall not live by bread alone, but by every word that proceeds from the mouth of God.

> Mark 4:7 (NKJV) Jesus said to him, '**It is written** again, You shall not tempt the LORD your God.'

> Mark 4:10 (NKJV) Then Jesus said to him, 'Away with you, Satan! **For it is written**, you shall worship the LORD your God, and Him only you shall serve.'

Now, knowing that God's words are THAT IMPORTANT and that Jesus used God's words against satan, let us also use God's words with authority!

Jesus taught us that whatever we SAY, we will have if we BELIEVE WHAT WE SAY in our hearts.

> Mark 11:23 (BLB) Truly I say to you that whoever shall say to this mountain, 'Be you taken away and be you cast into the sea,' and shall not doubt in his heart, but shall believe that what he says takes place, it will be done for him.

And remember, that the angels are employed when we release God's words.

> Psalm 103:20 (NKJV) Bless the LORD, you His angels, Who excel in strength, who do His word, Heeding the voice of His word.

So, use God's words when taking authority over the enemy!

Here is an example:

"Satan, God said I am His child (Romans 8:16)[2] and that I have full authority over you (Luke 10:19)[3] so I am casting you out of my home in Jesus' name, amen!"

Or I would say:

"Satan, I bind (Matt 16:19)[4] all your power over my family now and forever in Jesus' name, amen!"

"I loose (Matt 16:19) the blood of Jesus over my family now and forever in Jesus' name, amen!"

Or I would say:

"Satan, I cast you out (Mark 3:15)[5] of my body now in Jesus's name! The sickness you are trying to give me cannot stay on my body, for I AM the temple of the Living God and His Holy Spirit in Jesus' name, amen!"

(1Corinthians6:19)[6]

---

[2] Romans 8:16- *The Spirit himself bears witness with our spirit that we are children of God.*
[3] Luke 10:19- *Behold, I give you the authority to trample on serpents and scorpions, and over all the power of the enemy, and nothing shall by any means hurt you.*
[4] Matt 16:19- *I will give you the keys of the kingdom of heaven; whatever you bind on earth will be bound in heaven, and whatever you loose on earth will be loosed in heaven.*

[5] Mark 3:15 *and to have authority to cast out demons.*

And, with all the technology we have today, we only need to type into the browser search bar to find the scripture we need.

Here is an example:

Let's say I want to stop an argument; I would type in the google browser bar: 'scripture to stop fights.'

A link that says 'Six (6) bible verses to stop fighting' is displayed.

One of the scriptures is:

> Matthew 4:39 (NIV) He got up, rebuked the wind and said to the waves, 'Quiet! Be still!' then the wind died down and it was completely calm.

So, I would say it either aloud or in a whisper:

"Quiet! Be Still in Jesus' name!" until the fighting stops! I have personally used this scripture when I saw two (2) birds near me fighting, they stopped as soon as I started speaking those powerful words!

---

[6] *1 Corinthians 6:19 Do you not know that your body is a temple of the Holy Spirit who is in you, whom you have received from God? You are not your own*

CHAPTER SEVEN

THE FIRE OF GOD

God is a 'consuming fire' (Hebrews 12:29) and His fire is mentioned many times in the Bible.

> Exodus 19:18 (KJV) And mount Sinai was altogether on a smoke, because the LORD descended upon it in fire.

> Luke 3:16 (BLB) John answered all saying, 'I indeed baptize you with water, but the One mightier than I comes, of whom I am not worthy to untie the strap of His sandals; He will baptize you with the Holy Spirit and with fire'

> Numbers 11:1 (NJKV) Now when the people complained, it displeased the LORD; for the LORD heard it, and His anger was aroused. So the fire of the LORD burned among them, and consumed some in the outskirts of the camp.

We are also told that God's own heart is made of fiery stones.

And we know that Hell is 'where the maggots never die and the fire never goes out.' Mark 9:48 (NLT)

So, in my opinion, wherever the fire is, truth and judgment are not far behind.

Fire is also an element used to refine or purify things.

So, I use God's fire to purify my surroundings, my mind, and heart, my neighborhood, etc.

I use them in scripture like this:

"Father, I ask that you send your Holy Fire into my home to burn off any residue left behind by the enemy. Burn off everything that does not please you in Jesus' name! Amen!"

Or I say:

"Father, catch me on fire to cleanse my heart for your purposes! I surrender all to you in Jesus' name! Amen!"

It might be the same idea John Wesley had when he said: 'I set myself on fire and people come to watch me burn.'

I also ask the Father and the Holy Spirit to send Holy Fire into my computer wires or tv lines or into the atmosphere if I am having connection problems. Remember, the demons do not like fire because they know they will be cast into the Lake of Fire and tormented for all eternity.

CHAPTER EIGHT

THE LIVING WATER

The Living Water is not talked about much, but it is a part of God and His holy Throne!

> Jeremiah 17:13 (NLT) O LORD, the hope of Israel, all who turn away from you will be disgraced. They will be buried in the dust of the earth, for they have abandoned the LORD, the fountain of living water.
>
> John 4:10 (BSB) Jesus answered, 'If you knew the gift of God and who is asking you for a drink, you would have asked Him, and He would have given you living water.'
>
> Revelation 21:6-8 (NLT) Then He said to me, "It is done. I am the Alpha and the Omega, the beginning and the end. I will give to the one who thirsts from the spring of the water of life without cost.

The Living Water also is the same Crystal Sea of Life that flows from God and His throne.

> Revelation 22:1-2 (NLT) Then he showed me a river of the water of life, clear as crystal, coming from the throne of God and of the Lamb, in the middle of its street. On either side of the river was the tree of life, bearing twelve kinds of fruit, yielding its fruit every month; and the leaves of the tree were for the healing of the nations.

The Living Water has been given to us when we were saved and became the new creature in Christ! It comes through our newly created Spirit man, and we release it out through our bellies as an act of our will!

> John 4:14 (KJV) But whosoever drinketh of the water that I shall give him shall never thirst; but the water that I shall give him shall be in him a well of water springing up into everlasting life.
>
> John 7:38 (NLT) He who believes in Me, as the Scripture said, 'From his innermost being will flow rivers of living water.'

I believe this Living Water from God comes out of our bodies when we release it, just like when we release the Anointing!

> Isaiah 35:4-6 (KJV) Say to them that are of a fearful heart, Be strong, fear not: behold, your God will come with vengeance, even God with a recompence; he will come and save you.
>
> Then the eyes of the blind shall be opened, and the ears of the deaf shall be unstopped.
>
> Then shall the lame man leap as an hart, and the tongue of the dumb sing: **for in the wilderness shall waters break out, and streams in the desert.**

So, I release the Living Water through my home, my property, my atmosphere, and my neighborhood, to release God's healing, for blind eyes to be opened, deaf ears to hear, hard hearts to be softened, etc.

I say:

"Father, as your word says, I have the Living Water inside of me (John 7:38). I release this Living Water now into the ground on which stand so it will soak into the ground to touch every home in my neighborhood, my city, my state, my country and to infinity in Jesus' name! Amen!"

CHAPTER NINE

SPEAKING IN TONGUES

Even though in some churches or denominations this is a big controversy, I personally believe in tongues, because I can speak in tongues!

I did not even know about speaking in tongues until I started studying the bible as an adult!

Growing up, I was taught that the early church in Acts 2:4: 'All of them were filled with the Holy Spirit and began to speak in other tongues as the Spirit enabled them' was only a way God spoke to other nationalities of people in and around the area. So that everyone would hear about God in their native language.

I was also told that this does not happen anymore and that speaking in tongues is no longer appropriate.

But I have found the following scriptures on the subject:

> 1 Corinthians 14:2 (NIV) For anyone who speaks in a tongue does not speak to people but to God. Indeed, no one understands them; they utter mysteries by the Spirit.

> 1 Corinthians 1:5 (BSB) For in Him you have been enriched in every way, in all speech and all knowledge.
>
> Mark 16:17 (NIV) And these signs will accompany those who believe: In my name, they will drive out demons; they will speak in new tongues.

And, I see through scriptures, that not everyone understands words spoken in tongues:

> 1 Corinthians 14:4 (NIV) For anyone who speaks in a tongue does not speak to people but to God. Indeed, no one understands them; they utter mysteries by the Spirit.
>
> 1 Corinthians 14:28 (NIV) If there is no interpreter, the speaker should keep quiet in the church and speak to himself and to God.

So, I believe, that if everyone cannot understand what I am saying when I am speaking in tongues without God's wisdom and understanding, then neither can satan!

So, I use my ability to speak in tongues a lot! Just as Paul encourages us to do!

> 1 Corinthians 14:5 (NIV) I would like every one of you to speak in tongues,
>
> 1 Corinthians 14:18 (NIV) I thank God that I speak in tongues more than all of you.

And I know that when I am speaking in tongues, I am allowing the Holy Spirit to pray through me without my input, which is always best!

> 1 Corinthians 14:13 (NIV) For this reason the one who speaks in a tongue should pray that they may interpret what they say. **For if I pray in a tongue, my spirit prays, but my mind is unfruitful.**

> 1 Corinthians 13:1 (NIV) If I speak in the tongues of men or of angels, but do not have love, I am only a resounding gong or a clanging cymbal.

Now I did not start off speaking in tongues right away! I had to pray for it!

I would also listen to people in church services of ministries I know and trust when they started speaking in tongues during prayer services!

I would just start by loosening my tongue by repeating Ba, ba, ba, ba for a while.

Then I would start thanking God for His love in my native language, English!

I would start thanking Jesus for being my Savior, I would start thanking the Holy Spirit for being in me and with me!

I would do everything I could to keep my mouth moving with my voice engaged for Him to be able to take over!

Then finally, after many weeks went by....one night I was praying in my room with a church service on TV and my son came into my room.

He asked, "What language are you speaking?" because he could not understand what I was saying.

I laughed and said, "Tongues from God!! Hallelujah!!"

That is when I KNEW I was in the spirit of God! That is when I realized I could not understand the words coming from my mouth! But my spirit rejoiced!

And now I speak in tongues all the time; while I am driving, cleaning my home, mowing the lawn, etc!

I even sing in tongues! It makes me feel like an Italian opera singer!

And I found out later, that I can literally read while praying in tongues, since we do not engage our mind when we are speaking in tongues!

How awesome is that? Very awesome to me!

So, I recommend praying and learning to speak in tongues! I literally walk around my home speaking in tongues to coat my atmosphere. Because I have been taught by many spiritual warfare teachers that speaking in tongues clears out all evil!

Why?

Because when we are speaking in tongues, we are speaking words directly from God's Holy Spirit!

And we already KNOW that God's words are the MOST POWERFUL words ever!!

And I believe that when they hear tongues spoken aloud, they KNOW that God's Holy Spirit, the most powerful Spirit ever, is speaking, so they run in fear not knowing what God is declaring in this place!

CHAPTER TEN

ADDITIONAL KEYS

Here are more keys I use, to take back dominion:

1.) <u>Praise</u>

   I start to praise and thank Abba Father, King Jesus, and the Holy Spirit for my authority in Jesus! I thank them for the victory I have already!

2.) <u>Worship</u>

   I start to worship by dancing and singing victory songs to Father God and Jesus!

3.) <u>Laughter</u>

   I start to laugh at the devil! I ask him if that is all he has, then I laugh more!
   I say aloud, "For every moment your still here, I will tell one person about Jesus today!"

4.) <u>Verbally Deny Access</u>

   Say aloud that you are denying all evil access to you, to your family, to your home, to your neighborhood, to your city, to your state, and the like. Deny access to your things, your body, and so on.

Tell him and all his camp they are not welcome anymore and that you are the new Sheriff in town! You are the authority that is backed by all of Heaven! Backed by God, Jesus, and the Holy Spirit!

5.) <u>Loose the Host of Heaven- God's Angel Armies</u>
I loose Heaven's Host to shred the enemy and every stronghold and platform the enemy has built!
Then, I lose Century angels to stand guard in my home, on my property, at my workplace, and the like, so the enemy cannot come back without facing a fight!

I truly believe that this is the way that the Ecclesia will be

'which the gates of Hell will not prevail against!

I pray that each and every believer starts taking back their God-given, Jesus fought and bought authority to dominate this earth together with God, Jesus, and the Holy Spirit today, in Jesus' mighty name! Amen and Amen!

www.ingramcontent.com/pod-product-compliance
Lightning Source LLC
Chambersburg PA
CBHW060226050426
42446CB00013B/3188